To Brian And Gail –
Two Dear Friends,
With Love
Steve

It's A Good Thing, Too...

By Steve Zukmann

Illustrated by Kelly McMahon

PRICE STERN SLOAN, INC.

Los Angeles

Library of Congress Cataloging-in-Publication Data

Zukmann, Steve, 1949–

It's a good thing, too—.

Summary: In this sequel to "It's a Good Thing," brief text and humorous illustrations demonstrate why it's a good thing animals are the way they are.

1. Animals—Juvenile humor. 2. Wit and humor, Juvenile. [1. Animals—Wit and humor. 2. Wit and humor] I. McMahon, Kelly, ill. II. Title.

PN6231.A5Z854 1987   818'.5402   87-25863

ISBN 0-8431-2225-0

Copyright© 1987 by Steve Zukmann and Kelly McMahon

Published by Price Stern Sloan, Inc.

360 North La Cienega Boulevard, Los Angeles, California 90048

ISBN: 0-8431-2225-0

To Jenna,
Who brings life to life.

It's a good thing . . .

cats don't fly.

It's a good thing . . .

gerbils don't read the newspaper.

It's a good thing . . .

goldfish don't chew bubble gum.

It's a good thing . . .

beavers don't like to surf.

It's a good thing . . .

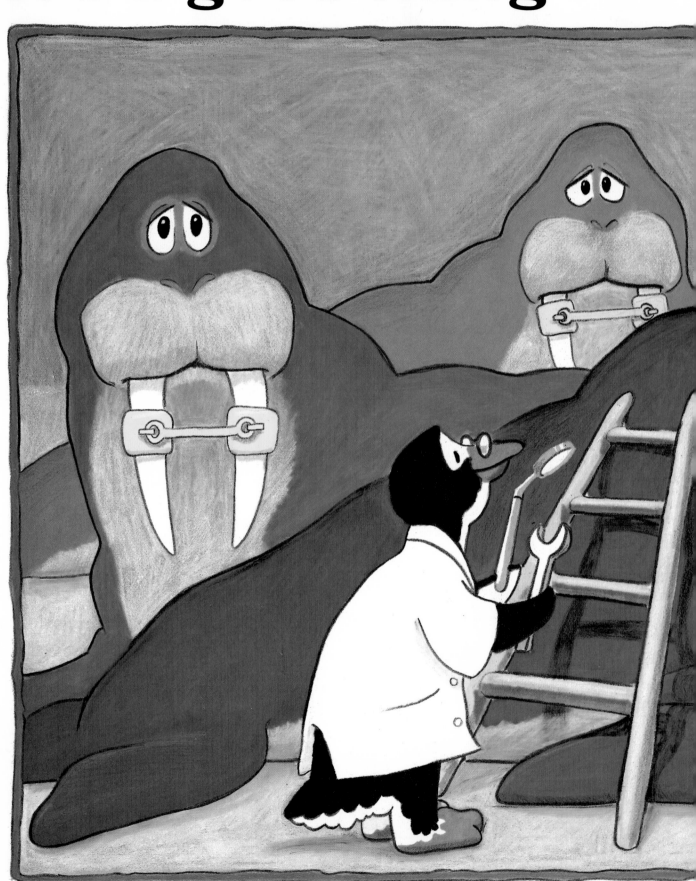

walruses don't wear braces.

lamingos don't take ballet lessons.

It's a good thing . . .

bison don't play football.

It's a good thing . . .

rabbits don't go to the movies.

It's a good thing . . .

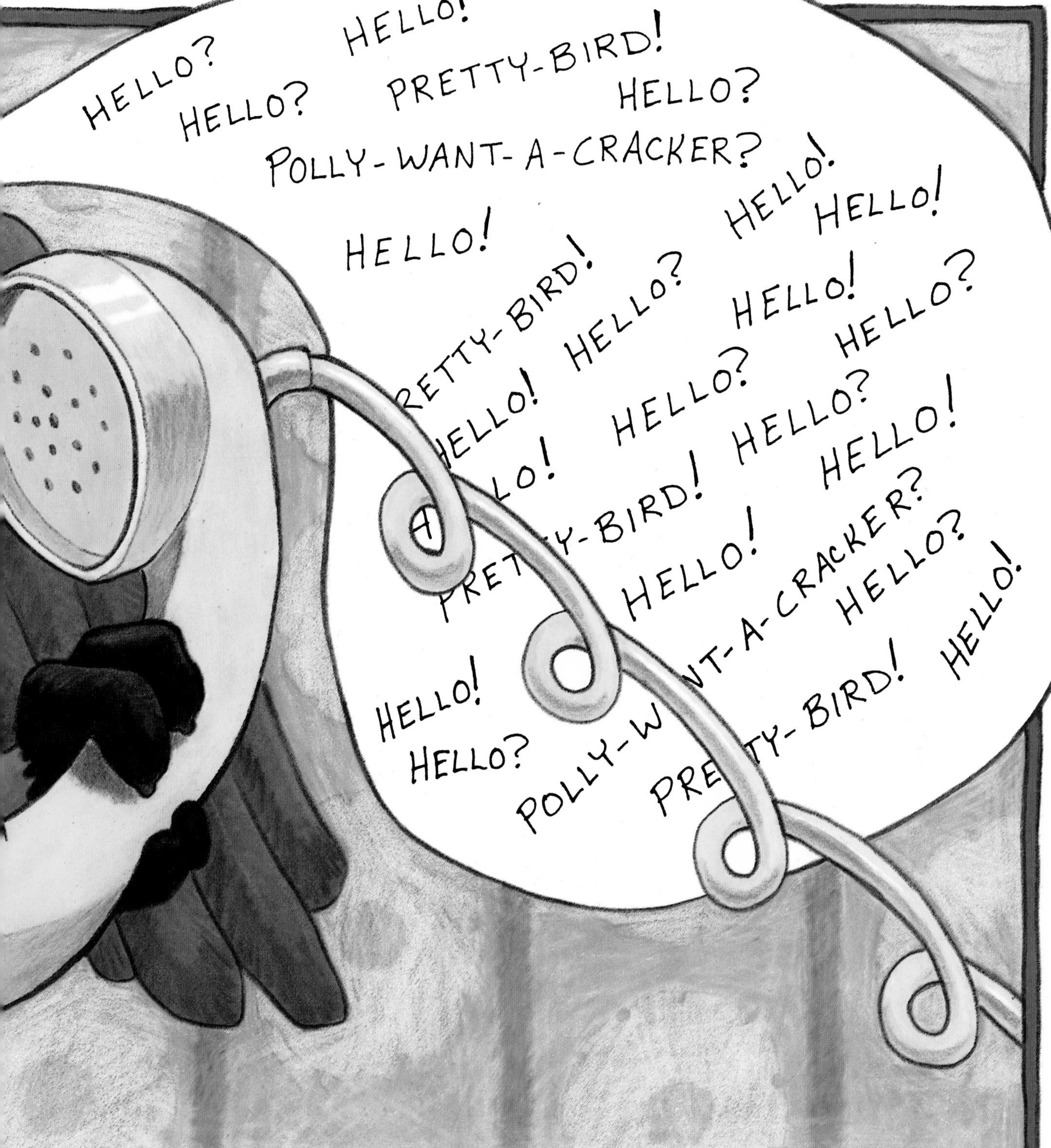

parrots don't answer the phone.

It's a good thing . . .

dogs don't drive cars.

It's a good thing . . .

horses don't play peopleshoes.

It's a good thing . . .

monkeys don't serve ice cream.

It's a good thing . . .

peacocks don't play hide and seek.

It's a good thing . . .

camels don't kiss.